Swaying on the Elephant's Shoulders

Swaying on the Elephant's Shoulders

Diana Woodcock

Little Red Tree Publishing, LLC
New London, Connecticut

Cover illustration: Charles Bleick

Text layout and Cover Design: Michael Linnard
Fonts used are Minion Pro and Ariel

First Edition, 2011, manufactured in USA
1 2 3 4 5 6 7 8 9 10 360 15 14 13 12 11

Previously printed poems are listed on the "Publication Credits" page at the back of the book.

All photographs used in this book, other than those specifically attributed below, are in the public domain.

The photograph of Diana Woodcock, at the back of this book and on the back cover, was taken by Markus Elblaus, VCUQatar photographer.

Woodcock, Diana.
  Swaying on the elephant's shoulders / by Diana Woodcock. -- 1st ed.
    p. cm.
  Includes Index.
  ISBN 978-1-935656-12-8 (pbk. : alk. paper)
  I. Poems. II. Title.
  PS3623.O664S93 2011
  811'.6--dc22
                              2011029311

Little Red Tree Publishing LLC
635 Ocean Avenue,
New London Connecticut 06320
www.littleredtree.com

CONTENTS

FOREWORD

It is with great pride that Little Red Tree presents the inaugural award of the Vernice Quedobeaux "Pathways" Poetry Prize for women to Diana Woodcock for her collection, *Swaying On the Elephant's Shoulders.*

This wonderful book of poems was greatly admired by all those involved with the selection process and was chosen by the final judge, Richard Harteis as the ultimate winner. In his introduction, Harteis explains the reason for his decision with perceptive insights into the poet's craft and unique voice. He cites examples that illustrate Diana's immense talent as a poet and as a human being with a fully developed spirit. He points to her concern for the victim, the oppressed and the discarded. He admires her curiosity and the degree to which she has walked the wide world, as well as her ability to make the foreign and the exotic available to us.

I think it is appropriate to take this opportunity to introduce the reader of this wonderful book of poetry to the person who inspired the competition, Vernice Quebodeaux. She was born in Egan, LA (on the banks of the Bayou Plaquemine Brûlé) in 1929. After an idyllic childhood spent in a small rural community, she emerged from high school ready to take her place in the world. Unfortunately, as she became an adult she struggling with repressive societal mores and family expectations, dysfunction, death, estranged children, family feuds, bigotry, apathy, abusive husbands and indifference to her writing aspirations. Despite and through it all, Vernice continued to write, and although being published in local media was encouraging, she failed to achieved her cherished goal of being a published poet and reaching a wider audience.

After her death the beginnings of a book of poetry called "Pathways" was discovered by her daughter, Tamara Martin, among her papers containing just 10 poems. These poems, along with others that survived from the many that where written but discarded in her moments of despair were incorporated into a book, *Sundays in the South*. Although only a small selection, they show Vernice's passion and concern for humanity and nature. In one poem she describes the sad conversations with old class mates whose childhood aspirations were never realized, the "...dreams that they had shelved!" We hope this prize in her name will help keep her dreams alive and those of other poets as they struggle to translate the world for us.

Therefore, with the award of the Vernice Quebodeaux "Pathways" Poetry Prize, we wish to honor her life and recognize the unique voices and challenges women poets face.

Diana Woodcock is a poet we feel sure Vernice would have enjoyed meeting and reading. We feel confident that this book will give immense pleasure to readers who are interested in meeting new poets of such excellent quality and appeal.

Michael Linnard,
Little Red Tree Publishing, 2011

AKNOWLEDGEMENTS

I am grateful to Gregory Donovan and Talvikki Ansel for their advice and encouragement, and to my Tibetan students in Lhasa who taught me an invaluable lesson about the precious gifts of peace and freedom. I also thank Charles Bleick, former Associate Dean at Virginia Commonwealth University in Qatar-School of the Arts, for the artwork on the cover. Special thanks to VCU Qatar's Faculty Research Committee for grants to pursue research, and to Vermont Studio Center and Virginia Center for the Creative Arts for fellowships and unfailing hospitality that gave me the space and time to craft and revise these poems.

INTRODUCTION

The Grace of Gentleness

In his remarkable book on shamanistic healing, Alberto Villoldo points out that a crucial initiation for central figures in the major religions requires a retreat from the world to achieve illumination. Jesus, Buddha, Mohamed all emerged enlightened through meditation and isolation. Somehow the silence and stark beauty of the desert enabled them to rediscover the world and reclaim it with spiritual authority. Diana Woodcock is another voice singing to us from the wilderness of Qatar, translating the world for us, calling us to a higher order, and like Adam and Eve in the garden, tasked with naming the bright world so that we may own it.

When I began the introduction for this manuscript, my heart sank a bit when I read, "*Swaying on the Elephant's Shoulders* expresses a three-fold concern for human rights, refugees, and ecology." I have been trained to believe that poetry usually fails to the exact extent it attempts to preach or instruct. There are notable exceptions, of course, such as Robert Bly's anti-war poems, or Muriel Rukeyser's early feminist poems (and those of a generation of female poets that came out from underneath her coat, as it were, like Maxine Kumin, Adrienne Rich and Dianne Wakoski to name a few,) and gay poets from Whitman to Ginsberg.

The subject of poetry, of course, is everything - human or divine, but how one treats the subject defines the art of poetry. And a reader who picks up a collection of poems, which has won an "international poetry prize for women," may be a little wary. Is the criteria to be poems written by women or poems written about women? Does the sex of the poet qualify the contestant or the philosophy of the poet writing about women? Most women no longer accept the term "poetess...." In any case, there are many fine poems that treat women's issues with a deft hand, one of the best of which is "Footbinding." It is a beautifully understated indictment of this practice and the Chinese treatment of female children, ending ironically with a young grand daughter squirming to squeeze herself into dresses several sizes too small.

I'm mostly with Valerie who holds that one makes poetry with images, not ideas, however. And Woodcock seems to be in this camp as well when she quotes Marilyn Chin in an epigraph to one of her poems:

> "*The poet guards the conscience of society–*
> no; you're wrong; she stands lonely on that
> hillock observing the pastures."

It is this talent for observation that is one of Woodcock's most striking qualities. And throughout the poems she is consciously aware of her role as observer. In "Survivor," which Mark Strand selected for inclusion in Best New Poets 2008, she describes, "Five cormorants on the decaying pier allowing me to watch them watching for fish, shadows under shadows on the water." Interestingly, the reader becomes a participant in the game, observing her observing the cormorants observing the fish. One thinks of a Renaissance master playing with perspective when he paints and we observe a woman looking through a window onto a courtyard which leads to a view of the valley below.

In "Hakeem's Farm," she expands her insight into observation when she says, "Always a strange sensation: awareness of the making of a memory." The ability to stand outside oneself and observe the world with compassion comes from the practice of meditation which seems to be an integral part of Woodcock's spiritual discipline and cultural background. Throughout the poems, she strives for such enlightenment and alludes to Buddhist practice. In "Choosing a Desert," she offers a signpost for a world-weary pilgrim:

> "In the silence and solitude, you'll learn to
> love your neighbor for who he is – not
> for what he says or claims to be. In this harsh

place, you'll find within yourself the grace of gentleness."

Woodcock does not don the habit of a Buddhist nun, though she seems to be a secular acolyte to our Lady of Sorrows. The desert is "...the place to enter the cloister of your own/design – take all the time you need to simply be."

Swaying on the Elephant's Shoulders is the journal of a soul who has not given up, who finds the world awesome in the truest sense of the word. She is not a saint - this book prize does not aim to canonize her, but she has not given up hope and continues to relish the beauty of the bright world, despite the horrors humanity persists in concocting. She hasn't grown cynical, is trying simply to be a good person, to understand, and forgive in the context of life's great moral complexity, a good example of which is the extraordinary poem, "The Pol Pot Soldier Tells His Side." Because he realizes his comrades will cut out his heart and force his victim to eat it, he butchers the pregnant woman to prove and save himself. After such troubling gore in the poem, the last stanza ends with a stunning, understated, surrealistic image:

> "We left them there
> under a camphor tree.
> I was the one who looked back–
> My compatriots had their stomachs set
> on finding crayfish for lunch.
> I saw the dead woman rise up
> to cradle her infant; glancing up
> from eating my heart, she looked at me
> with my mother's eyes.

It's hard to think of a poem that uses motherhood to greater effect in describing the fog and horror of war.

These poems are heartfelt, but Woodcock does not wear her heart on her sleeve. The poems take rise in a lyric impulse, but she realizes that a poem is a well-crafted object, as well as a cry from the heart. Woodcock transforms "raw" emotion into what T. S. Eliot calls artistic emotion, re-creating the original emotion in the reader through metaphor and the music of poetry. She is a good example of the new formalism and in the collection the reader will find many traditional forms such as the Ghazal, the Sonnet, Haiku, free verse, and concrete poetry. In one surprisingly successful experiment she re-tells the same poetic subject in three different poetic forms. In a deceptively simple poem, "Macau Teahouse" she sits among the old men drinking tea, honing her craft, sure there wasn't anywhere she'd rather be:

> "Sharing a table with canaries
> and old men, I would consider modulation,
> music and meaning while marking stresses
> and counting syllables on my fingers. They
> meanwhile, would debate ruthlessly
> whose bird was truly the sweetest heard."

After more charming detail on life in the cafe, the final line, "Why did I ever leave" hits the reader with an impact similar to the famous stark dictum that ends Rilke's poem on Appollo: "You must change your life."

In one of the many poems in which the poet visits a temple, we hear A Taoist recluse playing a bamboo flute. A lotus pond, the Chestnut Moon, draw her in. In the sky,

> "Fungi rose up from decaying
> cumuli, elixir-bound.
> Sounds of three rivers converging
> and metal chimes merging
> the portions of the day
> urged me to stay in seclusion,
> to leave behind every illusion
> of secular life."

The poem ends almost as a lullaby:

> "Crickets crouch
> at day's end
> in crevices near
> dying embers."

It would be nice to meet this woman one day, unlikely as that is. Her life experience is so interesting, the quality of her thought so attractive, her moral compass so true. But we have the poems. How lucky we are that she did not stay in seclusion, but continues to walk the wide world and listen to the music of the crickets.

Richard Harteis
West Palm Beach, May 2011

For my mother and father,
and in loving memory of Jean Vaughan Waldrop
(1926-1998)

Mirabai, or Mira Bai or Meerabai, was a 16th century princess whose life is known more through legend than verifiable historic fact. She was an aristocratic Hindu mystical singer and sahajiya (apasampradaya) devotee of lord Krishna from Rajasthan and one of the most significant figures of the Sant tradition of the Vaishnava bhakti movement. Some 12-1300 prayerful songs or bhajans attributed to her are popular throughout India and have been published in several translations worldwide. In the bhakti tradition, they are in passionate praise of lord Krishna.

*"I have swayed on the shoulders of an elephant,
and now you want me to climb on the back
of a jackass.?"*
—Mirabai

SWAYING ON THE ELEPHANT'S SHOULDERS

Swaying on the Elephant's Shoulders is a collection of poems expressing a three-fold concern for human rights, refugees and ecology. Each poem captures one of three states of readiness as the narrator is either poised to fly, held back, or drawn to the light. Each poem seeks to lend balance to the universe as it portrays the anguish or the joy of humanity and the pervasive sense of wonder available to us all. These are poems inspired by refugees, people living under communist rule, and fragile cultures and ecosystems on the brink of extinction. This collection, devoted to the threshold where silence and language meet, is an effort to promote worldwide justice and caretaking of the earth. It is a celebration of life, a protest against violence and greed, and an exploration of humanity's relationship with and interdependence upon nature and fellow human beings.

Diana Woodcock, 2011

PART I

POISED TO FLY

Sandstorm about to engulf the Pyramids.

DREAMING WE'RE TRAVELING THE WORLD AGAIN

"This is the wonderful thing about art, it can bring back the dead . . ."
Lynn Emanuel

You are alive again, so we decide
to make the most of it. We get off the train
in Ulan Bator (I think because we didn't before—
we hurried past, bound for Moscow).
Your hair's soot gray from the train's open window,
but you don't seem to care—you climb
onto the camel's back. A bouquet of miniscule
lavender blue wildflowers sprouts from your backpack.
I whisper, *Hide them! They're stolen*
from the Burren's crevices! You've been subpoenaed
to court! But you don't seem to care.
You call to me, *Our yurt is waiting.*

Across the steppes we drift aimlessly,
like fair-weather cumulus in a deep blue sky.
The camels sway and spit till by and by we're
in a sandstorm between Alexandria and Cairo,
sun obliterated, sinking fast. A staticky rasp
from the taxi driver's radio: ruh BAH buh music
drowns out the sirocco's roar. You stop
to wash your hair in a porcelain bowl
beside a rocky shore. Dingle Bay.
Somnolent boobies with blue feet rest beside you,
flown all the way from the Galapagos.
Nearby, I build a fire from peat.
You ask why. I reply, *To fill hot*
water bottles for your cold feet.

At last you stand alone on a Leningrad street.
Your cone has crumbled, fallen from
your hand. But you don't seem to care.
Vanilla ice cream melts over the pavement
into the shape of Corfu, expands until it stretches
into miles of warm white sand where once
we walked along the bluest ocean.

THE POL POT SOLDIER TELLS HIS SIDE

In no way did I let on
that I might want to put down
my machete and stop the others.
They would have me killed me
on the spot, cut out my heart and
thrown it to the wild dogs that
trailed us, or made the woman eat it
before cutting the fetus out of
her womb. They would have left
my body to rot among the canebrakes.

So I offered to do it single-handedly,
to prove myself. I stood over
the whimpering woman, raised
my machete and brought it down
into the mound of flesh that could
no longer protect the life growing
inside of her. Brought it down
into my own mother's womb,
into my own pre-natal sac,
into my own heart that was split
apart by her scream.

We left them there
under a camphor-tree.
I was the one who looked back—
my compatriots had their stomachs set
on finding crayfish for lunch.
I saw the dead woman rise up
to cradle her infant; pausing from
eating my heart, she looked at me
with my mother's eyes.

Old Camphor Tree growing on the side of a grassy hill.

"Gang of Slaves journeying to be sold in a Southern Market;" illustrates the domestic slave trade in the U.S. in September, 1839, a few miles from Fredericksburg, Virginia.

HENRY BOX BROWN

The idea came to me one day as I twisted
tobacco in the factory, grieving for family
sold and sent away to North Carolina,
remembering the slave coffle leaving
Richmond—heavy silence broken now
and then by a low whimpering and a clang;
my wife chained to the gang, holding her head
high; the wagon hauling away our children,
their eyes swollen with tears:
Go get a box and put yourself in it.
I decided I'd rather suffocate
in a crate three feet by two
and be settled in my grave
than go on living as a slave.
The trip by rail, if it went well,
would take nineteen hours or more
Richmond to Philadelphia.
If I survived, I would rise
up singing.

A large man, nearly two hundred pounds,
I climbed into that pine crate like one
about to be hung. I brung along crackers,
water in a beef bladder, my hat
for a fan, a small gimlet for boring air holes,
the memorized words of my favorite hymn,
my fear of dark, cramped spaces.
Prayed harder than I'd ever prayed as they
nailed down the lid and wound five hoops
of hickory wood around that box.

Chin resting on my knees, eyes peering
into the void, I faced my fear of
suffocating, drowning. Endured
strange pains suffered on the upside-down
journey to trainside, the clumsy transfer

to the wooden side paddlers at Aquia Creek,
eyes nearly swollen out of their sockets,
choke of my swallowed screams,
the slightest bit of air through pinpoint holes,
cold sweat on the steamboat journey—
wrong side up again, the tumble to the ground
as stevedores tossed me down, the crack
of my neck, another darkness—
inside my head. I suppose I slipped away,
breaking the mortal chains as I lay scrunched up
in my tomb, my spirit rising then and there to possess
the Promised Land.

Finally, the barge transfer: fishy smell of the
Susquehanna and Delaware; a voice announcing
my arrival in the north where freedom tolled for
every man. I heard whispers—they thought
I might be dead. A tapping on the box, *All right?*
All right, sir, I said. I heard the saw and hatchet,
the cutting away of five hickory hoops,
the prying off of the lid.

Wet with sweat, I rose up
from that pine box, singing,
Out of the miry clay!
After that day, everyone called me
Henry Box Brown.

"The Resurrection of Henry Box Brown at
Philadelphia," a lithograph by Samuel Rowse
published in 1850.

SURVIVOR

For Ngawang Sangdrol, Tibetan nun, released after eleven years

I walk beside the lake, late afternoon, waves restless and seagulls drowsy in sun along its shore. Five cormorants on the decaying pier allowing me to watch them watching for fish, shadows under shadows on the water. If I hold a sprig of rosemary to my nose and inhale deeply, for a moment flesh will not burn. The chinaberry tree with its wrinkled stone tells of its own hard journey: pride of India transplanted here; its transformation imminent—fragrant purple petals on slender stalks. The otherwise useless chaulmoogra yields an acrid oil that eases leprosy. Once, at the foot of a live oak, I broke down and wept. Acorn cups were scattered throughout the woods, turned up by the gods to catch rain for squirrels and quail to drink. All things find their place. I come back to settle before the fire, drawn like the pandora sphinx moth to the candle in the window. I slice the carambola into five equal pieces, five cormorants on the pier, five women screaming, five beatings each day, and the cattle prods. The Chinese prison guards went home at the end of their shifts to wives and daughters. A phantom orchid in moist pinewoods feasts on forest duff—the fungus in its roots a saving grace.

Hero-City Obelisk, Vosstaniya Square in St. Petersburg at 11:00 pm at night. This is an example of the "White Nights" of St. Petersburg when the sun sets for just a few hours at night but is never completely dark. The Obelisk was installed in May 1985 on the fortieth anniversary of Victory Day, WWII.

WHITE NIGHT

The name had changed once again
by then, Lenin no longer in vogue.
I can't remember the year, though I'm
sure I boarded the train before midnight,
a midsummer white night to be exact,
with a silvery light lingering over the streets,
embankments and the Neva, the Arctic Circle
only a few miles north, St. Petersburg on its forty-
four islands, Pushkin losing his life in a duel there,
Dostoyevsky sentenced to hard labor,
the Nazi nine-hundred-day-long blockade,
thousands dying of starvation,
the War Victims monument with its warning,
No one is forgotten, nothing is forgotten.

I was bound for the Polish border but
unwilling to leave, so when he hesitated there
in the doorway of my compartment, grasping
his one small suitcase, dressed in his soldier's
uniform, a half-smile on his face, I knew
even as I reached for my Russian-English phrasebook
and he began settling in that we would not be
sleeping through our one white night.

HOMESICK

He doesn't mean to be ungrateful,
one of few allowed to come here. But
claustrophobic among Chicago's skyscrapers,

Tenzin craves the taste of yak butter tea,
the melodious sound and pace of his native
tongue, the fire ceremony to smoke out dark

spirits. So he goes back to the skeleton dance,
to fragile mandalas made of sand.
The horse goes on wheels now.

The iron bird flies.
In the furthest land of the
red faces, he still dreams

of the home he's never seen:
Potala Palace, Himalayan peaks
rising above green-clad soldiers.

Exile—India, now America—
lands of the red faces,
fulfillment of ancient prophecy.

Potala Palace is located in Lhasa, Tibet.

The goddess A-Ma, (informal way to refer to Mazu (literally "Mother Ancestor"), also spelt Matsu), is the indigenous goddess of the sea who is said to protect fishermen and sailors, and is invoked as the patron deity of Southern China and East Asia.

OVERNIGHT FERRY, MACAU TO GUANGZHOU

Even as the taxi driver raced over
back alley cobblestones,

even as I oafishly jumped aboard
though the ferry had pulled out a foot
from the dock that wobbled and rocked
as if it actually were the spot where four
hundred years ago the goddess A-Ma
from Fukien had placed her slippered feet
to lend her name to Water Lily Peninsula,

even as I lingered on deck till Macau's lights
blended into one miniscule speck,

even as I considered that the average
passerby would have been hard pressed
to guess it was the Las Vegas of the Far East
there on the Pearl's umber mouth,
caressed by estuarial currents,

even then I knew I would leave her for good,
and one day come to savor each fact
and detail of place that might help me face
the moment's mediocrity.

SNOW LIONS

"Unless we enjoy ourselves,
others will make us suffer."
(Tibetan adage)

Viewed from Verde Valley, the San Francisco Peaks
loom like the Potala Palace over Lhasa, white
as the Harvest moon and snow lions.

Though the mountains inspire my drive,
Sedona to Flagstaff—healing and pure—
I am homesick for the ringing of temple bells.

"Music is for happiness," the old monk said,
smiling with his entire face, not a trace
of bitterness. Took me to the cemetery
late one night. Bells and hand drum,
chanting in unison, rhythm of voice and
instrument, monks confronting night spirits,
calling forth Yamataka to destroy death.

When resentment and hatred tempt me,
I don the black hat, dance as the old monk
instructed, bring my right palm to my left,
and pray.

Approaching the three extinct
volcanoes, I envision the Potala
filled once more with laughter.
Between blue sky and white peaks,
snow lions prevail.

In Tibet, the snow lion represents unconditional cheerfulness and a clear, precise mind that is free of doubt.

The square in front of the Jokhang Temple, Lhasa, Tibet.

FOR LHASA

March 17, 2008 I could not shake
the thought of you in flames.
Throughout the day whispering
the names of those I know still
living in your center, on your
periphery. Felt your misery.
Smelled burning shops, overturned cars,
Chinese flags. Saw smoke rising

incense-like over the Potala and Jokhang.
Heard the rumblings of a hundred
tanks moving through your hallowed
streets. Remembered the soldier
who narrowly missed me, knocking
me down—bicycle and body sprawled
on the ground as he sped past laughing.
Today I said it out loud to no one

in particular, to the nameless faces
in the crowd, "I never left you nor
loved any city more." So tonight
I'll fill seven prayer bowls, make
a mandala out of Arabian desert sand,
remember as I dangle my feet in Gulf
waters the source of the Ganges,
and wonder if indeed I am a certain

lama's reincarnation. I'll take that
long flight back, walk the famished,
enflamed road leading to the holy city
where I'll rise up like incense, a faithful
wife burning on her husband's pyre
because I can't forget you, most
fragile tragic city of Tibet.

TAUNGYI

When Grandmother dies for lack of attention—
negligence on the part of nurse or doctor—
I recall small ivory moths, three or four,
floating in my soup as I dined with a mountain
family far from Rangoon.

Christmas, the air was crisp.
Mist enveloped the village at dawn,
smoke from cooking fires at dusk.
The sparrows and wrens looked American.

Guiding the delicate drowning moths
to the edge of the bowl as talk turned
to politics, the need for satyagraha,
I took notes. Their grandmother died
for lack of treatment days before my friends—
smugglers of eye glasses, books, medicines—
began their mission.

We change the world one decision
at a time. The village people responding,
Ah, this too, now.

Twenty years, ten thousand miles later,
eating in the hospital canteen,
a moth floats in my soup. I reflect,
Ah, this too, now.

PAPER SON

Gazing at Grandfather's photograph,
I recall he was a paper son,
resident of Angel Island,
worker on the railroad.
His last five years he sat, eyes
vacant, throughout the day—

lured outside only for dim sum
on a Saturday or Sunday.
No longer took his songbird
to the park called Golden Gate.
Merely eight when he came alone
to America, he left parents and childhood

behind. Showed me once his treasured
book: Wongs' Genealogy. Thirty
generations. When I turned thirteen,
he wanted to take me back. "Why
should I go?" I rudely asked, afraid.
At nineteen, I walk through rice paddies

to the village west of Guangzhou where he
was born. Nothing speaks till I find familiar
lion heads stacked up in the corner
of a musty shop, and on one gray wall
of my great aunt's home a photograph of
me at age eight. On the back I'd written,

I can't wait to come to China.
I give her a recent one from college
graduation—and the one taken of
Grandfather before he died last year.
With nothing left to fear, I bring back
five generations to America.

Kuan Yin, a name that signifies her compassionate nature, literally meaning "'One who hears the cries of the world."

FEAST OF KUAN YIN, GODDESS OF COMPASSION

Compassion overwhelms me
as I watch two sea anemones battling
each other—tentacles flailing,

soft bodies pumped full of toxins.
The victor possesses the rock;
the loser slinks away.

Ancestors who
gave me muscle and nerve—
Earth's first predators.

Silence between what I am,
what I have been.
The limpid sea bears me back.

The calligraphy, "Silence-Thunder," evokes the essence of Zen practice.

This calligraphy, "Compassion."

BUFFALO STEW

The confessions:
pregnant women tied to trees,
machetes cutting out fetuses;
children killing their own parents
for stealing food; rats eaten raw.
How could I stomach them?

I listened, I heard like that bird just
there with its blank stare.

Exaggeration? I wish.
The Khmer Rouge, malaria, shadows
of vultures. One day a grandmother described
her childhood lush and wild. Closing her eyes,
she smiled and died. It made me go.

The old man squats in the shade of Ankhor
Wat, ruins rising from the jungle.
Cassia and basho trees sway in the breeze.
Children, women cut open here—so much
that cannot hide under the shadow
of the banana leaf the child carries,
riding his water buffalo, which—
at the end of its life—is sacrificed
for buffalo stew.

Angkor Wat, the magnificent temple complex at Angkor, Cambodia. It was built for the king Suryavarman II in the early 12th century and served as the state temple and capital city. It is considered the largest per-industralized structure in the world.

PART II

HELD BACK

DREAMING THE NIGHT BEFORE
LEAVING FOR AUSTRALIA
AFTER THE DIVORCE

A haggard black cat—
dab of moonlight
under its chin—brings me
a baby garter snake
curled tightly in its mouth.
Beyond sunflowers, a cornfield.
Jackdaws circle and caw.
I sit alone with my Walkman

beside a babbling brook,
watching dabbling ducks—
mallards, perhaps.
A man in a hat made of straw
paints the scene in between
eating fat strawberries.
Suddenly a gunshot, a scream.
Dusk turns to starry night.

The ducks quack louder while a junco
repositions herself on the nearest branch.
I ask if she's drawn near to jeer
at flightless, lifeless me, or to hear
Mozart's Magic Flute filtering through
cypress trees. Flexing her wings,
she suggests in perfect English,
though with an Australian twang,

Come fly away with me
down under. I say, Why not?
But then, I can't fly. She asks,
Have you tried?
Now the black cat won't let go;
it's dug its claws into my back.
And the snake, grown fat,
has wrapped itself round my neck.

View of the Topkapi Palace from the Bosporus.

TURKISH CARPET

With a trace of dread, I've dragged
the tree of life out from the dark of two years
closeted, unrolled it and spread it out
beside the bed--its birds of meadow root red
and indigo, so long ago the two of us
in Istanbul, on the Bosphorus
in Cappadocia with its lunar landscape—
pyramids and monoliths of white volcanic rock,
monasteries hollowed into cliffs,
Konya's whirling dervishes, the muezzins' calls
to prayer echoing across the towns at dawn

We stood inside the Gates of Happiness
in silence, walked wordlessly in the gardens
of Topkapi Palace where turtles with lit candles
on their backs once meandered among tulips
tulips to amuse the sultans; wandered like mutes
among mosques, tombs and marbled ruins;
leaned on all that's left of Artemis' temple:
a lone column in the middle of a swamp;
stopped to rest, speechless, along the Black Sea coast
in an orchard of hazelnuts; strolled voiceless
through a village—narrow lanes, meandering sheep—
where disks of dung hung drying on the walls
of mud-brick houses.

In that country part East part West,
on that bridge between Europe and Asia,
we felt the impenetrable divide and began
the arduous work of goodbye.

ON THE EVE OF THE DAY OF ATONEMENT

The Mojave aster blooming on time again
lines roadsides and desert slopes.
Squirrels dashing, even leaves swirling
across the path cause me to slam on brakes,
afraid of killing anything on Yom Kippur,
this autumn of our latest war.

Once I sat in an orange grove
along a dusty dirt road midway
between Alexandria and Cairo.
Taxi driver bribed to veer off the
highway, I glimpsed village life
far from tourists and pyramids.
A man in a white robe invited me
into his grove—peeled and served me
oranges as if I were long-awaited, then
took me home to meet his family.
Sat on the floor of their one room hut—
drank water from a common cup.

Years later in Lhasa circling the Jokhang,
a child thrusting her hand into my purse.
Pushing her away, I made her sway and fall,
then kept on walking beside temple walls
past chanting monks, grazing yaks,
prostrating pilgrims, bulging sacks of rice,
and old women spinning prayer wheels.

A typical orange grove on the road to Alexandria from Cairo.

White Tailed deer.

CASUALTY

The deer he hit in the predawn
on the deserted road outside Austin:
it broke him.

He took up his gun, considered how
long the body would lie there exposed.
Kneeling, he pulled the trigger—
only the bluebonnets and winecups
to witness.

A year had passed since the crash
in a snowstorm of the medevac plane—
white with blood-red crosses on its
wings. Three days for the search teams
to find them.

He had traded his shift that day—
he, the suicidal one, while none
of his coworkers leaned that way.
Their bodies had melted into the
winter sun warming ponderosa pines
and those volcanic peaks—Humphreys,
Fremont and Agassiz.

He had kissed his wife goodbye without
smiling, the slightest peck on the lips,
the neighbors' dogs barking.

FEAST DAY, LADY OF SORROWS

For the cameraman, he waves a hand
over his parched land—all dust and wind,
not a tinge of green anywhere. He hasn't seen

a harvest in two years, while across the border
poppies bloom—soon to seduce the West.
He's sold his roof to buy food to feed his family

six weeks at best; he's sent his smallest son
to rob the rat's hole of its grain.
At this point I stop eating my bisque—

I can't seem to swallow the shellfish.
I turn off the TV and sit in the dark on the
deck watching the waning Hunter's Moon

rise above my gable roof, listening to
rasping crickets and the winds of war
as they spin out of control, wondering

what I'm willing to sell, who to rob
to endure the banishment from the garden.
All these repercussions: bloated stomachs;

glossed over eyes; roofless homes;
adolescent robbers of rats; parched
land; poor bone-dry Tajikistan.

The Hunter's Moon—also known as blood moon or sanguine moon—is the first full moon after the harvest moon, which is the full moon nearest the autumnal equinox.

The roof of the Jokhang Temple, Lhasa, Tibet, with the Potala Palace in the distance. The Potala Palace was the home of the 14th Dalai Lama prior to his departure as a consequence of the Chinese invasion.

WISH FOR FREEDOM

From the doctor's window, I glimpse the autumn sun
descending abruptly behind a snow-crowned
pinnacle, but only after it sets afire the faces

of maroon-robed monks circling the Jokhang Temple.
They move without hurry like mist
hovering above the river at dawn, apart

from the listless throng of pilgrims and peddlers.
The swishing of their robes whispers,
          We Tibetans wish to be free.

The doctor tells me they sent him
to the mines north of Lhasa because
he had relatives in America.

Says he treated them equally: Chinese
soldiers and his fellow Tibetan prisoners.
Smiling, he recalls rooms heated by embers.

Here in Lhasa it is colder, he says,
though further south, because there is
no coal, no wood to burn.

But here, I remind him, the sky is clear,
the night reveals a barrage of stars within arm's reach.
And he's found a wife to keep him warm.

Can you hear the wish? he asks me.
I hear nothing else as it ripples across the plains
of the Changtang and back to the flat rooftops

of the Potala where once the Dalai Lama stood
watching his people play and dance and sing
as maroon-robed monks circled the Jokhang Temple.

THE HOUSE WREN AND THE SWALLOWTAIL

I sit at dusk under a ylang-ylang tree,
drinking, of all things, Oswego tea.

How can the wren emit such songs, melodic and calm,
yet puncture others' eggs—kill their young?

"It's Darwin you'll have to ask," the wren sings, then hands me
a custard apple and begins trilling again—sweet enough to obtain
a plenary indulgence.

As the wren creeps into a cranny for a cutworm, a tiger
swallowtail appears to lay her spherical egg on a leaf of the tulip tree.

Did the thistle's nectar or the allure of the wren's sweet song
draw her here, and where has she been?

"Coursing up and down canyons all day," she yaps with her wings.

"What a life," I say.
The swallowtail insists it's not all roses, or in her case, lilac and pipevines.
She lacks a jaw, the fluttering never really stops.

I say, "But still, if you ask me to come with you, I will,"
ready to raise the screen and fly.

The Eastern Tiger Swallowtail butterfly.

North face of Mount Kailash, Tibet. The Tibetan name for the mountain is Gangs Rinpoche.

SHANGRI-LA

Feeling it was time (finally believing
what Tibetans say one must believe
to survive the cold and storms along the way),

though I was far from being pure of heart
(to enter Shambala one must be sure one is,
they warned), I trekked to the sacred mountain

between red-tasseled yaks carrying sacks of salt
to trade in India for rice, among pilgrims who
gently nudged flies away and possessed faith

that one circuit around Mt. Kailas cancels out
the sins of a lifetime. In the midst of the multitude
celebrating Buddha's birthday, monks positioned

the prayer pole, and I felt myself vanish into rock faces
honeycombed with abandoned mud huts two thousand
years old. Felt myself dissolve into a land where even

flies and fleas must be spared, then rise on the wings of
unspoken chants that spun and finally flung themselves
from hand-held prayer wheels.

Thirteen days circling the temple, slipping away to meditate
inside caves darkened by the day-long shadow
of the Himalayas. When I returned to earth-bound life,

I would often recall standing tall and longingly,
at length—though my heart was far from pure—
on the threshold of bliss.

APHRODISIAC

Along the serpentine road
Shanghai to Chengdu,
two rare gifts from the San Diego
Zoo—Southern White rhinos—
died. Who knew, except for
swifts and shimmering mists
that witnessed it, if they had succumbed
to heat and dehydration as reported,
or been butchered for the sure-fire
erections promised in their pale horns.

In Kowloon: a sultry, musty apothecary.
Pharmacy shelves of tiger bone pills,
saiga antelope horn, bear bile capsules
costing twenty times the street price
of heroin, a Cape Fur bull seal's penis
ground up and labeled aphrodisiac.

At the bar next door, beery-eyed Chinese
men in the smoky din watching thin
prostitutes—some home-grown, some
from the Philippines—in their tight
jeans, painting their pale lips red.

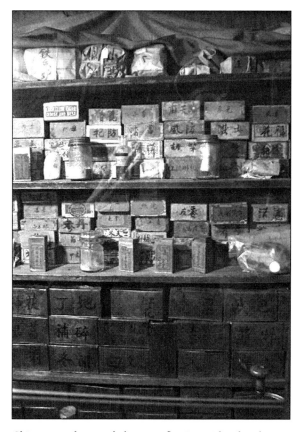

Chinese apothecary shelves overflowing with aphrodisiacs, cures, potions and remedies in card and wooden boxes, and tin cans handed down the centuries.

Ruins of St. Paul's Cathedral, Macau, by George Chinnery (1774–1852). The cathedral was built in 1602 and destroyed by fire in 1835. Only the southern stone façade remains today.

VENICE HAS HER PIGEONS

Venice has her pigeons: rock doves
  diving down to appeal to meandering strollers,
    dotting the timeworn stones with snow.

But here on China's southern coast,
  who fills the sky at sunset
    and cries out over this ancient enclave?

    Macau has her swallows.

The Galapagos have their blue-footed boobies
  strutting about like circus clowns,
    tempering, enlivening the sky and ground.

But here beneath the Mainland,
  who brightens up the ashen skies and cobblestones,
    and blends its song with city drones?

    Ngou Muhn* has her sparrows.

China has her Peking ducks
  grazing in the countryside,
    billowing like clouds of rain.

But here where the place name means city of God,
  who waits stately in its cage—
    a meal on some back alley lane?

    Macau eats her owls.

*the Chinese (Cantonese) word for Macau

TENTATIVE ADVICE FROM A WEARY TRAVELER

Would I advise you to do it—scatter
your affections in places so set apart
from what you have known that your heart
can find no way home?

Would I say get up at dawn and follow the truck
collecting the dead of Calcutta curled up
as if sleeping on the sidewalks?

Would I suggest you book second-class seats
on the train, Banares to Agra, and stare
into eyes reflecting the pain of platform beggars
station after station?

Should I say follow the prostitutes of Patpong
for a day and curse the Western men who've traveled
halfway round the world to sleep with them?
Then stay as long as the monks allow at the monastery
on Lantau? Spend at least a season strolling the seven
hills, the cobblestone lanes of Macau?

Would I advise you, once you return and settle down,
to plant bamboo, though it will spread like kudzu—
relentlessly prodding you to sponsor panda bears
endangered in those misty mountains of Tibet
and Sichuan, to sketch faces you can't forget
from the Land of Snows?

Tibet: Land of Snows.

Red Admiral butterfly on a nettle.

THE OTHER WORLD

The withes of river willows waver
between yellow and green. I offer one
to the skeen of parting geese passing over.
Easy these days to express straightforward

sentiments, the season paring down to lean.
The strings of my zither broken now.
Gone the one who understood and sang with me
my songs. How many more autumns to bear?

How much longer to waver my willowy arms
in the air and mock at death, to wait for renascence?
Stillness and gloss of the river, scent of decaying
leaves everywhere, mist rising, light of the Hunter's

pearl-white moon shining on the oxeye daisy.
How she loved them all—willow, geese, river, moon,
daisy. We worked and dreamed and sailed the ocean
together, clung to the notion we could save the world.

Silly girls, believing it would always be that way.
Sleepless with grief, I reach for the answer,
long for unbroken silken strings so I can play
until the first birdsong of dawn.

Red admiral on the nettle, you settle there as if
fully aware your midsummer days chasing
painted ladies at dusk are gone.
Winter here with me, please. West wind,

wild geese, no letters from far away.
Whispered words like Taoist talismans
sent, but the recipient cannot leave her
other world to return.

CHENGDU, BESIDE THE BROCADE RIVER

No poet these days could thrive here—
coal haze reducing the sun to a smear,
the paulownia tree covered in coal dust,
polluted waters failing to evoke Xue Tao's
handmade paper for brushing brief poems,
sky as gray as the habit she wore her
final years.

Tang dynasty woman, Taoist recluse,
I hear you singing of lush bamboo,
scattered peonies, solitary cicadas.

Boatwoman passing by, may I
catch a ride and read to you from Xue's
yongwu poems while the Hunter's Moon
spreads its ivory gown over the mountain-
laced Sichuan basin?

Ousted from Tibet, I too write poems of protest
and banishment—longing for a life of solitude,
her courage to retire from serving wine
and writing poems for the elite to follow
Tu Fu's example.

From the River Gazing Tower, I see no jade
white dust—no scattered peony petals
on the snow—only coal-gray particles thrust
out of chimneys and falling on the shoulders
of men and their songbirds in cages, on the pages
of the book of poems, which the young woman
with her one long braid is reading
beside the Brocade.

Statue of Xue Tao, (770 - 832), in Wang
Jianglou Park, Chengdu, China.

River View Pavilion Park (Wangjianglou Gongyuan)
overlooks the Jin River (Jin Jiang, or "Brocade River"),
with the four-story Qing-era pavilion (River Gazing
Tower) almost 100 feet tall.

A view of the mountains on the road from Peiko Tso to Saga,
just north of Saga, Tibet.

FALLOW FIELDS, GATHERED HARVEST

Fallow fields, gathered harvest
are flung-open gates to truths whispered
among fallen leaves. Same for frontier towns
and borderlands of exile, steppes and sparse
grasses-----hard for me to look at now,
still harder to view mountains in paintings
as peaceful when memories come: cold
and stinging wind. Tibetans took me in.

Back home now in the West, I clumsily
practice calligraphy with my bamboo brush
from Guangzhou, imagine I am the scroll's
fiery painted dragon-horse who races
to the places sun and moon go-----caparisoned
in rich brocade, feeding on dried jujubes.

In the marketplace back East, one corner
reserved for caged birds: vacuous parakeets
and parrots with beaks as orange as the carrots
piled high in the opposite corner between
persimmons and pale green lemons.

I scan Western rafters now for swallows'
nests, praying for good fortune.
Tenderly taking a tiny moon in my hand,
I envision the oyster from which it emerged,
imagine myself on the verge of weaving
among lotuses in the midst of golden fish
whispering their truths.

GWAI LO

Tangerines
pyramiding
in the marketplace,
chestnuts steaming in
a vendor's portable fire
on the corner across from
the Temple of Kuan Yin.
Paper-whites perfuming the
air, whispered words here and
there gwai lo and bok gwai (foreign
devil, white ghost—syllables as brittle as
burnt toast) as I walk by. Suspicion in
the eyes of the widows dressed in black.
I feel them watching my back, resist the urge to
tease by asking in perfect Cantonese, Neih sihk
jaw fahn meih ah? Have you eaten yet? I've learned
well how to greet those I pass, but I haven't learned
to ignore their icy stares. Mutely I cry out, I'm not like
the others; I've come in peace to seek the mind, the heart of
compassion. Is there no other way to find it? I inquire of the
goddess whose temple I've entered now. Incense and golden glow of the
Buddha behind glass. I exit past one woman deciphering her future in the
toss of jossticks, buy seven chestnuts and the compassion of three tangerines,
one bouquet of paperwhites to screen the accusations and get me through a
cold night.

SUDDEN GRACE

A crow caws from the deck just now,
glisteningly wet from morning rain.

I promised I wouldn't complain
when my luck ran out. But I tell him
anyway how I long to get my charmed
life back, no breathtaking view to
wake up to these mornings:

no rising sun singeing the edge
of the Himalayas, no
South China Sea leashed
by mist to the sky, no
sound of the erhu drifting
from my neighbor's bamboo grove.

Only days ago, the trees lifted up
on each blossom's cupped sail; now
the dogwood petals lie scattered
over the rain-soaked trail.

Lost in thought,
I miss my turn-off,
circle again through the woods
along the lake. Which is why
I see her: lone doe grazing
in the glade. I've never met her
there before—a sudden grace,
like the crow's caw.

The Terracotta Army or the "Terra Cotta Warriors and Horses," is a collection of terracotta sculptures depicting the armies of Qin Shi Huang, the first Emperor of China. They were buried with the emperor in 210-209 BC to help guard his empire in his afterlife.

THOUGHTS AFTER MEETING A FRIEND'S ADOPTED DAUGHTER FROM XI'AN

Notes of a lute drift from the bamboo grove.
One warrior, wrapped in his battle robe,
squats and cocks his clay head. Another

stands and pulls his bow taut.
China's first emperor, the despot Qin,
defended himself against death with ten

thousand warriors. Burned books and scholars
but shunned the feudal tradition—women,
slaves, soldiers buried with their masters—

took terra cotta in place of flesh and blood.
Each face given its place in time: one gazing
skyward; one eager to kill; one frightened by all

he cannot know. Horses stand ready to bolt.
Warriors' lips, furled and thick, oppose
those of women found only in paintings:

delicately thin—each one a minikin with bound feet.
On a school outing, little emperors without siblings
bend over the edge of the massive tomb.

No girls among them.
Staring into the pit, they count bowmen,
infantrymen, chariots in their rows.

Jade encircles the thin wrist that will drip
blood onto the lute's strings before the full
moon sets. Undaunted by fear, she whose

baby girl has been torn from her breast
faces death with grit and grace—
not a trace of Qin's battalions.

FOOTBINDING

In the marketplace of Macau, an old woman
with three-inch feet totters on the curb,
struggling to climb four-hundred-year-old
cobblestone steps.

Dressed in black, gray hair pulled tightly into a bun,
she's been most of her life a refugee
without papers—on the run from injustice.
Trailing behind her like a shadow, a nightmare,
scent of jasmine in the stifling humid air
are those memories of childhood:

eight toes bent under, bandaged tight, drawn
toward each heel till bones would finally yield.
Now the golden lotus shape of each foot haunts her—
flaunts her pain, subservience, ironic privilege.
Reminder of a sister's death from rotting flesh:
feet bound for a slow journey to the next world.

No school for her, so assiduous she had to be
with the business of being female:
misshaping feet, waking from her childhood dreams
at thirteen to serve husband in place of father.
Some mornings she still awakens gasping

for air, reaching by habit to loosen the phantom
bands of cloth wound tightly around her toes,
feeling the throes of pain—constant sleet—as they
curve under the balls of her feet. Persistent
memory of dreading the dragging of her body
across the floor to do chores while brothers
ran and played.

Now she grimaces as her granddaughter
refuses to eat in the marketplace
and squirms to squeeze into dresses
several sizes too small.

Very young Chinese girl wearing lotus shoes after her
feet were bound.

Yamdrok Tso Lake is one of the three largest sacred lakes in Tibet.

TIBETAN BUS DRIVER

Some faces stay with us—forever caught
in the rearview mirror, toothless grin
reflected again and again with the hand-rolled
cigarette near its end dangling from those lips,
the red-eyed glance cast over his shoulder
as he took yet another chance around the next
hairpin curve, each swerve to avoid hitting
peasants and their yaks unnerving.

Boarding his dilapidated bus as it idled in the pre-
dawn dark, stark beside the Jokhang Temple,
I allowed him to usher me into the front row seat.
From Lhasa to Shigatze—seven hours or more,
along the sacred Lake Yamdrok Tso,
across a wasteland of melting snow
marked by each driver's own choice of paths,
past mudslides slid back by smiling,
singing peasants wielding rusting shovels—
I placed my life in his trembling hands,

clinging to my wise friend's gift of a hot water bottle
as if it might serve as a life jacket should we go over
the next cliff and down the ravine, under the threshold
of the waves. Rushing downstream, who would hear
my frozen scream? Privy to a water burial reserved
for babies and holy men. Give me sky and vultures
when I die.

PART III

DRAWN TO THE LIGHT

SPARSE

Sparks scattered in the ground,
the seed begins its journey.
The dew grows cold. The Hunter's Moon
stalks fallow fields, rotting gourds.
Beside it, solitary Fomalhaut shines.
Gates between the realms
of life and death swing open.

Today a sleepy orange, last sulphur
of the season, dartled between three lingering
lantana blossoms on the wood edge—
my days just as numbered.
Titmice and blue jays squabble
at the birdbath as one cloud in the sky
becomes the baby wrapped in white,
floating down Lhasa's river toward her burial.

Unable to turn away that day years ago,
I chose to stay and watch the white bundle
diminish to a mere speck, then vanish.
On the riverbank, homeless peasants
and pilgrims with their yaks meandered
among tents and cooking fires, their children
playing games as the corpse passed by.
Too old for water burials, they all
would be given the sky.

In the east before dawn,
Venus and elusive Mercury
side by side. I am a seed,
a spark, a speck.

DRAWN TO THE LIGHT

As rain falls again, tapping
on tin roof and windowpane,
beading on bamboo leaves
into globules like so many

unnamed planets, who can
blame me for turning my back
on my books of pneumatic
realism and mysticism—soul

inflamed, water turned fire?
Lightning flashes above the
bamboo grove. Wood burns,
crackles, sizzles until it fizzles,

finally consumed by the stove.
Thunder makes its rounds—
who doesn't have ears to
hear within it the harmony

of the spheres? Cold dark rain
falling for millions of years,
consuming fire flaring up higher
and higher in perfect union.

And me, moth-like, caught up and
freed in the middle, partnering
the universe, drawn to the light
arising out of darkness.

KAREN AMONG THE KACHINAS

Some physicists say death frees our bodily atoms
to fathom new space, uncharted places, to
rearrange themselves into new forms of matter
that scatter and dance into the cosmos--the body
not God's design, His creations eternal.
The physical does not exist, they say. Only
the mind is real. When the body, ego, illusions
take leave, we live forever.

The great horned owl that flew into my plane
three weeks before my death knew my name—
I was just thirty-four: mother of two;
respiratory therapist; animal lover.
From the Navajo Bitter Water Clan
(half Navajo, half San Carlos Apache),
I could converse with sheep and horses,
roosters and people in pain. I went back
to my childhood haunts.

They say women from my clan are headstrong.
I was bent on flying—Mama said I was wrong
to go against Father's wishes. But now he says
I couldn't have died in a better spot: the plane
went down among four feet of snow,
ponderosa pines, and those intermediaries
of the deities who live on Flagstaff's peaks.
Still in their winter sleep, they had not yet left
for the Bear Dance ceremonies marking
February's false spring.

He prays every day now for such a perfect death,
imagining me communing with Crow Mother,
singing with Red Beard, dancing with Humming Bird
and Road Runner. *Father, you dance too,
I urge him. Dance to the music of the living
and the dead, and you will find your way home,*
my Lakota friend once said.

MANDALA

Are these the primary poisons: ignorance, hatred, greed?
Could a conch shell or a simple bell awaken me?
A lotus rooted in mud enlighten me with blossoming
energy? Blind me to all that is not sublime?

Could the sapient salmon swimming upstream nudge me
toward the wildest dream? The horse—graceful
source of strength and speed—lead me?
Could the tiger take my negativity? The dragon grant me
wisdom, fire? The eagle lift me up to shadow
rainbows to the celestial realm? How do I begin
to recognize yak-skin boots as sea lions disguised,
constraining negative traits?

You say level the earth? Subdue all evil
spirits? How? Could grass, if blessed,
really soften at last the homeward journey?
A rosary made of pearls protect me from
evil? Sing, you say, while tending the animals,
weaving, planting, harvesting. But how do I find
the words?

Be a chaksam-pa, you urge—build bridges. How?
Find God in music, yak and sun. But how?
Could I ever learn to play the dranyen and move
through life as if around a mandala,
balancing—always balancing,
ready to be erased?

Antiques shop in Macau.

MOMENTOS

Porcelain pillows, calligraphy brushes,
snuff bottles from Macau's antique shops
reveal a gentler time—notes of the pipa
resounding through bamboo forest,
mountain mists, spring showers.

I place them on a shelf near the Tsingtao
scroll inscribed with the character for silence,
hung on the most central wall passed
several times each day. I burn incense
from the Temple of Kuan Yin, mercy
goddess in a land that bound and broke
the feet of girls—and now has regressed
to killing or selling them.

I read the poems of Ts'ai Yen—
born in a time of peace, then
heaven's mandate was withdrawn,
forced to marry the enemy and live
ten thousand clouds and mountains
from her home. Exiled
from her heartland, surrounded
by her own momentos: notes
and smoke rising from the pipa
and sandalwood incense.

STREAKED-WINGED RED SKIMMER

One dragonfly lingers
on the brown tip of a summer
green reed like a flame
on a candle at mass.

Poison has spoiled its meal
of midges and broken its eggs.
The last of its kind
to inhabit this shoreline,

it hangs on,
burns in the mid-day sun,
purifying the day.
No longer skimming

its lake, it poses on its reedy
throne—a lone ember
glowing in the fumes
of Malathion.

The Streaked-wing Red Skimmer dragonfly perched on a reed.

YOU LAUGHED AT ME

"When we . . . get into the forests again,
we shall shiver with cold and fright,
but things will happen to us
so that we don't know ourselves."
  D.H. Lawrence

I (blank verse)

You laughed at me—asked why on earth I'd waste
a Saturday evening traipsing through the woods
calling to "trifling" owls, but there I was
in Appomattox standing in a glade
no longer lit with fireflies or moon,
bent on mimicking a descending, tremulous wail.
And then it happened: a lone screech owl replied
as if to appease me, adding a tiny trill
and the softest purr. I shined my light on her.
She'd come so boldly to the very edge of the woods,
and there she sat—she was watching me watch her—
her big yellow eyes two candles in the night.
You'll laugh, I know, but I'll tell you it was enough.
Later I heard the great horned and the barred,
and you should know I've made a pact to go back
as soon as the tiny saw-whet owl returns
to winter there, and I'll surely laugh all the while,
for the old insignificant things have crumbled.

II (a sonnet)

You asked me why on earth I'd waste my time—
a Saturday evening traipsing through the woods.
You said you wouldn't even waste a dime
to call to "trifling" owls; I said you should.
So I went all alone and kept quite still,
and mimicked as best I could a tremulous wail.
When finally the screech owl replied, I felt a thrill.
I spotted her at the edge of the glade near the trail
and marveled at her bold curiosity,
her eyes and posture seeming to imply
compassion and a humble probity.
I wished we'd never have to say goodbye.
I know when I tell you this you'll scold and laugh,
but I have decided I shall be going back.

III (a haiku)

Leaves fall and fade now.
I call; the owl answers me.
The stars glow brighter.

AMERICAN WOODCOCK

Early March.
Sunset.
Wheezing of the wading woodcock
has begun.
In courtship flight,
it spirals up, circles,
then plummets to the ground.
Chunky,
quail-sized,
large bulging eyes,
it hides—camouflaged
among dried leaves.
Whistling of wings
in the moist thicket.
The long bill
extracting earthworms,
probing.
Another spiraling flight
just before the fall of night,
and a feather drifts
within reach.

YEAR OF LHASA

Around the yaks' necks, golden flecks
of sunlight fall on timbrel bells. Leavening
the city with prayer, pilgrims arrive each day
in droves. Dust clouds rise like incense
off unpaved roads. Monks chant prayers,
making ritual stairs to heaven from palace,
marketplace and monastery. Rancid yak butter
tea stinks in musty shops and cafes.

Wind whimpers through cracks in the wall.
Bits of sod roof fall onto our bed. All day
the dread of sunset and the cold of night.
Daggerlike icicles cling to laundry hung drying
on the balcony. Two Chinese men play elephant chess
while keeping one eye on us, the range
of the Himalayas wrapped round us all—
stark and gray save for their snow caps, each peak
sharp as the angel shark's backward curving teeth.

All day pilgrims wind their way round the Jokhang
Temple, chanting and spinning hand-held prayer wheels.
Nowhere to go—this city always their destination—
they move in slow motion, some so old or sick
they've come to die in this sacred place.

Before nightfall, they settle by the river,
light their fires with yakpats, play homemade lutes
and reed pipes, drink butter tea while their yaks
graze and the haze of their fires rises like incense
over the river, drifting with their prayers and flashing
shorebirds on the shifting wind across the Himalayas
and the closed border to the exiled Dalai Lama.

Around the necks of the young girls, ivory
pearls of moonlight fall on stringed shells.
Every night every one of them dreaming
of that thousand-mile flight.

Osprey watches.

PESTICIDE SURVIVOR

An osprey watches me
from a high branch of the birch,
perched above the escarpment
beside the rushing river.

We keep still together,
neither disturbing the other.
Two red-headed woodpeckers
chatter incessantly while storing

nuts and acorns in dead tree
crevices. A bluebird passes by
like a sapphire flung from its setting.
When the shot rings out

on the opposite shore, we all four
flinch. My goal now: to leave
this earth without disturbing
a single blossom of clover.

PALE TIGER SWALLOWTAIL

"Who remembers the Armenians?"
    Adolf Hitler

I can't escape from being human,
but I can keep closer company
with other species—herd reindeer
in Lapland all year, or hibernate

as a hermit hidden in a labyrinth
of a canyon—observing raven
and gila monster, grieving
for Armenians massacred

by the Turks, for the Caribbean's
Taino killed off by Columbus'
men who, searching for gold,
lost their souls.

A Pale Tiger seeks hilltops.
Its yellow relative courses up
and down canyons all day,
flexing and curling its wings,

tied to the heat and light of the sun.
I can't run from being human.
Still, I'd rather be a Pale Tiger
or an Oregon Swallowtail.

A Pale Tiger Swallowtail butterfly.

Wild horses in the Rockies.

NEARLY MINE

"Peace be to earth and to airy space."
   Athara Veda XIX

Two tawny does bolted past today—
the closest they've come, though I've
often felt their eyes on me.

Now that the days are cold and short,
these have become nearly mine:
the deer, their woods, the leaf-strewn

trail that winds beside the river—
so few of my own species venturing forth.
Back inside, I watch a band of wild

horses in the Rockies,
avoid the news from the front lines,
long for big skies and the high altitude

of Flagstaff or Lhasa where, among
stars and elk and yak, airy space
became for a while nearly mine.

LAST DAYS OF SUMMER

Shifting my tack, I'm on the James
kayaking—the prickle of faces,
events and names I thought I'd forgotten
a waterfall cascading down,
the daily manifestos and roll-call in the camp,
one line for resettlement, the other
repatriation, smell of whiskey on the border
guards' breath, children playing with shards
of shattered glass, hard-learned lessons of
what not to ask—what became of Sok Noth,
and who shot the woman pregnant with twins?

No one wanted to hear, so I locked these things
inside—got on with my life till I no longer cried.
And Somoen's cough, tubercular in the night,
ceased coming back to jolt me awake—I
somehow could have slipped her the medicine
that would have saved her, could have adopted
the one whose smile was the most timid—whose leg
had to be cut off above the knee. Still running to me
in my dreams, he still screams for help.

I breathe deep, smell of fish and promise of rain
in the air, sunset rays with a flair converging
like railroad tracks. Only days till leaves fall
and the James freezes over. Cormorants nap
on the decaying pier, ghosts skimming the river.
Overhead, a blue jay chases off a hawk twice its size.

ENGLISH AS A SECOND LANGUAGE

They come after a long day
spent working in the sun,
smiling unremittingly as if
they still believe they've done
the right thing. I teach them
the basics, they teach me about
escape and new identities.

Weary of their brave facades,
gently, *Speak only English here*
from their countries that defines them.
Antonio from El Salvador offers us
shards of shrapnel taken from his side
the day he nearly died. Jose from Argentina
holds up a photograph of his father missing
for decades, and a memory that never fades.
As he slips back into Spanish, I remind him
gently, Speak only English here.
Khema from Cambodia's brought a wooden
spoon and her mother holding it over the fire
the day Pol Pot's men came at noon to rape
and kill her while the children sat hidden
behind the rolled-up sleeping mats.

After they've each had a turn, I say,
Tonight let's look at adjectives and practice
describing your dead and missing relatives.
The lesson goes quite well—combination ESL
and grief workshop.

When the class is over, I watch them
gather up all they've brought. Each one
has reverted to the first language. I watch
them walking to their cars. Their feet
are made of glass.

TIBET POEM

If I go out into the streets at dawn,
I will see how the pilgrims put on a new day—
how they spin their wheels to pray,
yaks at their heels, making their way
to the temple.

If I bend down and press my ear to the ground
at the place of slaughter, I might hear
the last words of a martyr.

If I write them down and swallow them
so no soldier can rip them from my hands—
no Red Guard tottering between homesickness,
whiskey and the party line can discard them
like watermelon seeds or orange rind,

I might feel them piercing—a sword inside me—
till once I've moved back west of Caucasus,
the martyr's last words will thrust themselves up
from my gut, slash their way out of my mouth
till the world is wounded by them.

BEYOND THE CLOUDS MOUNTAIN

Late autumn.
The ivy still climbing,
sun-bound, claret-
colored. Underfoot,

faded withered leaves and
memories. South of Chengdu,
on Beyond the Clouds
Mountain, a temple

once drew me in: a lotus pond,
the Chestnut Moon, wailing
gibbons, a Taoist recluse
playing a bamboo flute.

Diamond yellow willows
swayed in the wind,
tossing their weakened fibers
onto transparent currents.

Fungi rose up from decaying
cumuli, elixir-bound.
Sounds of three rivers converging
and metal chimes merging

the portions of the day
urged me to stay in seclusion,
to leave behind every illusion
of secular life.

Crickets crouch
at day's end
in crevices near
dying embers.

Drapchi Prison, or Lhasa Prison No. 1, is the largest prison in Tibet, located in Lhasa. Originally built as a Tibetan military garrison, Drapchi was transformed into a prison after the 1959 Tibetan uprising.

INTERVIEW WITH A TIBETAN SURVIVOR

For Ngawang Sangdrol

I was there the year you entered hell.
> *Could you describe that cell and having nothing*
> *but your life to lose?*

They say you sang Tibetan blues in the night.
> *Weren't you frightened the Chinese guards might*
> *awaken from their drunken stupors?*

I was teaching on the outskirts of Lhasa,
just down the dusty road from Drapchi Prison.
> *Did you volunteer, or was it always clear you were the*
> *strong one, too independent and spry for the role of*
> *wife, the one your family should give to Garu Nunnery?*

I'd ride past on my bike, wondering about the life inside those
walls—the morning wake-up calls, the bland thin soup, cold
cement floor, the threadbare flea-infested blanket. If I heard
your screams for help, what could I do? And now this interview.
> *Could you describe the cattle prods and other forms of*
> *torture, the sounds that broke the silence: approaching*
> *boots at midnight, chains that kept you company in the next*
> *cell gone silent, first bird song at dawn? And of you fourteen*
> *nuns who sang of your protest songs, how many died?*
> *How did you survive? Why unstoppable?*

Yes, you are right but too humble: we are all survivors—
of lost loves, failed marriages, broken dreams, our own follies
and mistakes. But you have arrived at these golden gates.
> *Could you tell me about the ones who didn't survive?*
> *Your mother died while you were in prison, yes?*
> *Would you describe her influence, your grandmothers' lives?*
> *How old were you when you realized your land was occupied*
> *by strangers?*

There are no guards outside your door now.
> *Why do you tremble so?*
> *Tell me what you hear*
> *down the hall, in the next cell.*

CHARMED LIFE

Even I don't always believe it all—
the life I lived before I took a fall:
hitching rides with elephants, sleeping in
bamboo groves where slanting moonlight
and frogs in droves would awaken me some
nights as if to say, *Don't sleep this one
glorious life away.*

Jade green sea and rice fields
surrounding me, the relentless calls
of spiraling gulls and hawkers in the streets,
     Jellied sweets and sticky rice!
(such ambrosial delights)
      Roasted tubers and chestnuts!

For a time my life was a delicate screen
through which the sun would stream. But
now I'm trying to hold on to the hope of
light that could thinly filter in past the dark
night that has swallowed me whole.

CHINA POEM

Mimosa blooms in the vacant lot
where an old man without shoes
stakes out his nightly spot.
Its fragrance will drive his dreams.
He is singing softly.
All's not what it seems.

The Red Moon rises—arouses life's
basic rhythms: seasons, tides,
breath, pulse of the wrist-vein.
In the soft summer rain, two toddlers
balanced in the twin buckets
of the water carrier smile at passersby.
The one bearing their load smiles, too.

Those smiles in the middle of miles
of nowhere—that song—compared to
empty stares, long silences between
complaints back home in the land of plenty.

The rain stops, each lingering
drop enhancing the fragrance
of mimosa.

MACAU TEAHOUSE

The old wooden teahouse leaned
toward the inner harbor, well-hidden
from new casinos and day tourists
rushing over from Hong Kong, Tokyo
and Taipei. Sharing a table with canaries
and old men, I would consider modulation,
music and meaning while marking stresses
and counting syllables on my fingers.
They, meanwhile, would debate ruthlessly
whose bird was truly the sweetest heard.

Drinking boh-lei or gok-fa,
eating shrimp dumplings and sticky rice
wrapped in lotus leaves, I would ignore
the spitting of bones onto the floor—
the loud slurping of noodles—sure
there wasn't anywhere I'd rather be.
For there I was: lover of birds and
Chinese tea, of things both ancient
and exotic, on the footstool of China
in a wooden house that had brought them
all together in a most melodic,
hypnotic way.

Why didn't I stay?

Macau teahouse.

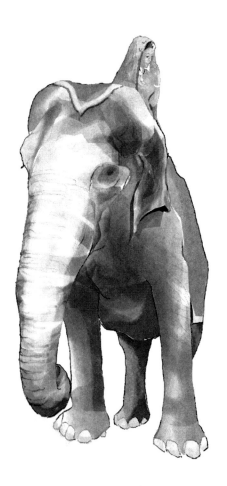

Illustration by Charles Bleick

BEYOND THE BACK OF THE JACKASS

She began to doubt that she'd ever really
swayed on an elephant's shoulders, and when
people would ask her about where she'd been
and all she'd done, she would reply, You've
got the wrong person; you've made a mistake—
I would never be brave enough to do those things
you say I've done.

Caught between magnificence and
insignificance, she became confused—
felt the Muse had turned its back on her.
Every room became a blur, a prison cell.
Every window had to be opened wide
to let fresh air inside, let out the ghosts.
Sensing some imprecatory presence,
she no longer bought flowers or golden carps
from the marketplace, no longer spent hours
by the river praising the grace of the otters
and the heron.

She put away her assemblage of writing
accoutrements—hid the bundle of manuscripts
and lists of writing tips deep in the bowels
of the basement. Not a pencil or scrap of paper
remained. Friends decided she'd gone insane.

She began to sleep more, dream deeper,
remember the smallest details. She walked
in the sun and rain, and little by little she
regained her soul. Became expectant again
of the impossible. Began to recall the lives
she'd lived—every frightening experience,
every enlightening moment. Began to see clearly
how the good outweighed the bad, how when
all was done and said, she had truly led
a most extraordinary life.

Everyone thought the worst was over,
thought any day she'd make her way down
into the bowels of the basement and haul out
her writing gear. But then the circus came
to town, and they say she was found

face-down after following the trail of elephants
from their camp to the fairground.
She had attempted to climb up onto the shoulders
of the last one in tow—had lost her footing
and fallen in the path of an approaching giraffe.

An unfortunate accident, everyone said,
but at least she had spent every last bit
of strength she had reaching beyond
the back of the jackass.

CHOOSING A DESERT

When you decide the time has come
for a move to the desert, consider this one:
peninsula with Arabian Gulf waters on three
sides, an inland sea, flamingos in the shallows,
songs of that Persian nightingale—the white-
cheeked bulbul—pure magical

incantations, the sidra tree spreading
its branches like arms raised in praise.
In the silence and solitude, you'll learn
to love your neighbor for who he is—not
what he claims to be. In this harsh place,
you'll find within yourself the grace of

gentleness. Sea lavender will draw you
to saline flats you might otherwise avoid,
moorhen and crakes to sewage lagoons hidden
by tall green reeds. You'll grow so accustomed
to arid flat tan terrain till you'll feel like an alien
in lush mountains and rain. You'll settle in,

but once in a while the cloud-moving wind will
stir the chords of vagabondage, and you'll long
for a mountain stream and the woodsong.
You'll thirst for rain—day-long rain, rain that
drenches dreams all night. You'll miss birches
and mushrooms though a seamlessness exists in all

this barrenness—a sand-brown transience that shouldn't
be missed: quiet inlets with gentle ripples, springtime
with Desert hyacinths blossoming, the season of
mists when desert scrub drips with moisture.
This is the place to enter the cloister of your own
design—take all the time you need to simply be.

Zubara Fort, Qatar.

HAKEEM'S FARM

Two hours' drive from Doha,
heading cross-desert northwest,
his family farm sprawls hidden
behind brick walls—waterfalls
music to the ears after the silent
shifting of sand. In this desert land,
I often dream of rain, but I always
awaken to the same blue sky, relentless
sun. On his farm, three camels come
to nuzzle me. There are peacocks,
ostriches, Arabian horses, ducks
and reems, deer from Australia,
cattle, goats, sheep. No pigs, of course.

My father started with nothing,
Hakeem proudly beems. *Now he owns
six businesses in town.* We sit down
to a feast—fresh fish from the Arabian Gulf,
vegetables and lamb from the farm.
I could understand if they'd known
we were coming, but here we sit unexpectedly.
I hear the ducks squabbling on the pond,
feel the nuzzling of the camels lingering on.
Always a strange sensation: awareness
of the making of a memory.

Just a few friendly words exchanged
at Zubara Fort. *Come see my farm—
you are welcome,* he had smiled, this young
man who had studied five years in Tucson,
then returned to his Bedouin roots.
Such hospitality in the desert: strangers
welcomed as if emissaries of God—a gift
that in the West has all but died. Money
can't buy happiness—how many have tried?
But at least in the middle of a desert a farm
that thrives and a feast fit for Allah.

A GHAZAL

How I long to be in the great silence!
I could live in the sea: in the great silence.

One could get lost in the Arctic's vastness—
get drunk on its purity in the ashen silence.

Watch the cardinal feed his mate in spring;
then tell me what you see in the green silence.

Snipers and child molesters remain at large.
We must set them free in the grave silence.

Mother Theresa held the dying man,
praying sincerely in the sorrowful silence.

Frogs and toads have burrowed under the mud—
they keep company now in the icy silence.

The mockingbird mocks loudly at midnight.
But soon it will flee into the reserved silence.

When the runaway slave was finally caught,
he was hung from a tree in the grim silence.

From the widow's walk, watch porpoises play.
Join the anemone in the majestic silence.

Let the leaves fall and the nights grow longer.
Diana's ready to be in the grand silence.

Dusk in the arctic summer.

The Atlas moth.

JUST FOR ONCE

Just for once
try being as fluid
as ice melting.
Cease bucking change.

Try believing
you have all you need
and your soul is immense.
Try simply seeing things

as they are,
watching without judging—
without fearing—
the cobra.

Try keeping as still
as the egret who stands
in perfect quiescence
among sacred lotus flowers,

and consider how the Atlas moth,
though its majestic wings stretch out
one foot in length, emerges to live
just one day.

RENDEZVOUS

"But ask the beasts now,
and they shall teach you."
    --Job 12:7

Sometimes even I think it must not be true,
but then I close my eyes and smile.
I remember our unexpected rendezvous—

how many miles we traveled I never knew,
with me admiring his unhurried style.
Sometimes even I think it cannot be true.

I was merely a young Western gentile who grew
weary of the West—fled to the Far East for awhile.
I remember our enchanting rendezvous.

But now in my own country I often feel blue—
as if I am an old homesick exile.
Sometimes I have my doubts it is true.

But I remember the jungle we meandered through.
And his shoulders—so broad and strong, yet mild.
I remember our chance rendezvous.

That elephant could have carried me to Timbuktu.
I pray I'll never become senile—
never forget, though it does seem too good to be true.
I treasure our tremendous rendezvous.

Indian elephant walking down a village path in the jungles of Northern India.

Thai villagers bathing two elephants in a local river.

KAMPUT

Through plumes of dust kicked up by the van
carrying me to a refugee camp in a no-man's-
land twenty miles now twenty years

down the road, I watched a Thai peasant splash
water on his elephant's sides and back—
its snorkeling trunk submerged. I'd made a vow

after visiting Dachau. One afternoon
young refugees danced and sang their ancient
Khmer songs; their elders strummed along on

homemade instruments, rehearsing for the night's
performance. Lunar New Year or Nirvana Day?
So long ago—I can't say. Would I have heeded

the warning bell if it had signaled me just then
to leave that makeshift town as the enemy gained
ground? That sense of belonging among them

never diminishing, nor the belief that if I had
deserted them, my life would have vanished
like plumes of dust into nothingness.

I COULD BECOME THE PHOENIX

For the wild thorns grow tame
And will do nothing to oppose the flame . . .
        Robert Lowell

I could become volatile and travel
on the air—become a thistle seed whisked
away by my bristly parachute of long
white hairs—if I would just stop clinging
to the earth.

I could laze all day:
a vine snake posing as a branch,
trading my culinary concerns
for a lucky chance at sustenance,
if I would simply accept whatever
comes within reach.

I could become the phoenix, or
at the very least wild thorns not
resisting the flame—not grasping,
not clinging. I could scintillate till
I finally ignite—phoenix-like—
from nothing more or less than
midnight tears' heat.

Sandhill cranes returning.

Cheung Chau (Long Island) is a small island southwest
of Hong Kong Island.

AS SANDHILLS CRANES WERE RETURNING
(In Memory of Tapey)

As Sandhill cranes were returning
to Platte River and the first cherry blossoms
were appearing in my country's capitol,
the Tibetan monk sat down in a one-meter

circle to pray and immolate himself.
In no time, he was absorbed into the mandala
of the solar system—white breath
and a somber relinquishment purifying

the air while those who witnessed it—
Chinese soldiers and Tibetans alike—
went home to crouch in corners of dark
rooms where they spun like spiders

their threads of dreams that life is more—
must be more—than what it seems.
In solitary silence far from processional
chants and military watchdogs, each one

believing with all his heart in the white
dove returning to the Ark. And in his grief,
each one transformed—set free in a one-meter
circle by the mystery of faith and truth.

CHEUNG CHAU

Once I stayed a month alone on an island lying out from Hong Kong. No cars allowed, I climbed up a narrow path—heavy pack on my back—into clouds. On the mountain's rim, overlooking the South China Sea, in a deserted Salesian retreat house—holes in the ceiling, every morning I'd wake up mist-damp and think I'd died in my sleep and gone to heaven. Then and there, in the island's humid salt air, I learned of my true calling: to disturb and awaken everyone I dared. And I watched every childhood dream of safety vanish with the passing junks and the setting sun and moon. Butterflies and bees winked at me from their beams of bright blossoms. At night, stars above and phosphorescent fish below vied for my attention. I had left behind every invention of modern man—spent my days in a blaze of sunflowers, watching how they turn their faces toward the sun all day and waves wash over the rocky inlet below. Nowhere to go, I did everything in slow motion—washing, eating, walking in the untended garden, reading even—only a few lines a day about the way of grace. I hung suspended between wild sea and sky, infinite space—a haven and a grace, the only liturgy I needed: prayer, song, homily all rolled into one—the sighing and hum of nature. And I leaned in close— turned my face sunflower-like dawn till dusk toward the sun. You should try it sometime soon: go hibernate alone on an island far from home. You'll uncover powers and magic you never dreamed you possessed. You'll pick out one junk on the South China Sea and create a camel—that ship of sands crossing the Arabian Desert. You'll enmesh yourself in a mysticism more intoxicating than the salt air you imbibe, more liberating than the beauty of the bamboo surrounding you. You'll hear the sound of water as the frog plops into the lily-strewn pond. Above you, blue sky. Below you, blue sea. Beside you, wild blue violets scenting grasshoppers' legs. Surrounding you, blue planet suspended in dark space. Meandering among lush, graceful grasses and vines, you'll commune with blue-jays, bees, pilot whales, crimson and purple sunsets—never once concerned with the fact that what the sky is giving back to your eye is ether waves— nothing more than a rhythmic disturbance in a field of force. You couldn't care less how many angstrom units line the distance from crest to crest. Cicadas and crickets will tell you bedtime stories. Angels will whisper to you of coming glories. You'll never want to leave. At least that's how it was for me.

Salesian retreat house, Cheung Chau, Hong Kong.

Oak Hydrangea blooms.

NINE YEARS LATER, ON INTERNATIONAL EARTH DAY*
(In memory of Jean Waldrop)

*"Then mock at Death and Time with glances
And wavering arms and wandering dances."*
                    – W.B. Yeats

Knowing nothing about pancreatic cancer—
how fast it spreads, how close she was to the edge—
I sent her Yeats' quote one month before she died.
Knowing her, she laughed and cried.

The oak hydrangea blooms today in the place
where she lived so many years. Dusk pale as pewter
spreads over her favorite lake. In her woods, her words
reverberate, "Let's emulate nature in December, in July."
Under the long-leaf pines, I let myself cry. When eyes
have dried, I read Neruda, "Life is what it's about;
I want no truck with death."

How she loved this earth—ocean and sea
especially, blue-footed boobies her babies—
she drew to herself all earthly things, as holy
persons do (if Bingen's Hildegard was right).

I stay all night, wondering if the one bird
of paradise blossom I took her two days before
she died opened in time. "The leaves are falling . . .
the heavy earth . . .from all the stars . . . we are
falling," Rilke's calling from the other side.

Don't try to catch me. Let the veil be lifted.
Let me, as she did, give my soul *with a smile
like a rose.*** Then, in grateful humble repose,
rise up to die.

*first observed 4/22/1970
**Rumi

INDEX

Poem titles are in bold, and the first lines in italicized text.

PUBLICATION CREDITS

Thanks are due to the editors of the following publications in which these poems, or versions of them, have appeared:

After Shocks: The Poetry of Recovery for Life-Shattering Events (English as a Second Language, Last Days of Summer),
Alligator Juniper (Fallow Fields, Gathered Harvest),
Anderbo.com (Karen among the Kachinas),
Atlanta Review (For Lhasa, Year of Lhasa, Hakeem's Farm),
Avocet (You Laughed at Me, The House Wren and the Swallowtail),
Best New Poets 2008 (Survivor),
Blue Fifth Review (Sparse),
Chrysalis (Mandala, published as Lessons from Tibet),
Creative Juices (Pesticide Survivor),
Creekwalker (Sparse, Just for Once, Streak-winged Red Skimmer),
Drumvoices Revue (Homesick),
Enigmatist (Gwai Lo),
Hampden-Sydney Review (Tibetan Bus Driver),
Hawai'i Pacific Review, reprinted in their Best of the Decade issue, 2007 (The Pol Pot Soldier Tells His Side),
Hobble Creek Review (Dreaming We're Traveling the World Again),
Homestead Review (I Could Become the Phoenix),
Istanbul Literature Review (Aphrodisiac, Buffalo Stew, Casualty, Feast of Kuan Yin, Goddess of Compassion, Turkish Carpet, White Night),
Kerf (Wish for Freedom),
Least-loved Beasts of the Really Wild West, (Streak-winged Red Skimmer),
Litchfield Review (Recitation of the Fatiha for the Dead),
Nimrod International Journal (English as a Second Language, Survivor),
Other Voices International Project (Henry Box Brown, Recitation of the Fatiha for the Dead, Snow Lions, The Pol Pot Soldier Tells His Side), *Pear Noir* (Cheurng Chau),
Pudding 39 (Venice Has Her Pigeons),
Quercus Review (Choosing a Desert),
Raving Dove (As Sandhill Cranes Were Returning, For Lhasa),
River Oak Review (Nine Years Later),
Rosebud (Tibet Poem),
Sandcutters (Momentos),

Small Brushes (Nearly Mine),
Susan B & Me (Footbinding, Interview with a Tibetan Survivor),
White Heron (Just for Once),
Wisconsin Review (Henry Box Brown).

The following poems appeared in *Mandala* (a 2010 chapbook):

Aphrodisiac,
Buffalo Stew,
English as a Second Language,
Feast of Kuan Yin Goodness of Mercy,
Footbinding,
For Lhasa,
Henry Box Brown,
Homesick,
Interview with a Tibetan Survivor,
Just for Once,
Karen Among the Kachinas,
Last Days of Summer, Mandala,
Nearly Mine,
On the Eve of the Day of Atonement,
Recitation of the Fatiha for the Dead,
Sparse,
Survivor,
The Pol Pot Soldier Tells His Side,
Tibetan Bus Driver,
Turkish Carpet,
White Night,
Wish for Freedom,
Year of Lhasa.

The following poems appeared in *Travels of Gwai Lo* (a 2009 chapbook):

Beyond the Clouds Mountain:
Chengdu Beside the Brocade River,
Charmed Life,
China Poem,
Gwai-Lo,
Kamput,
Macau Teahouse,

Momentos,
Overnight Ferry Macau to Guangzhou,
Paper Son,
Shangri-la,
Taungyi,
Tentative Advice from a Weary Traveler,
The Other World.

ABOUT THE AUTHOR

DIANA WOODCOCK

Although born in the United States, Diana Woodcock has spent the best part of her life living abroad—nearly eight years in Asia and the past seven in Qatar. In 2010 she won first place in the Vernice Quebodeaux "Pathways" Poetry Prize, by Little Red Tree Publishing. Her third chapbook, *In the Shade of the Sidra Tree*, was published in 2010 (Finishing Line Press). Her first two chapbooks were published in 2009: *Mandala*, by Foothills Publishing as part of its *Poets for Peace series*; and *Travels of a Gwai Lo* by Toadlily Press, whose editors nominated the title poem for a Pushcart Prize. In 2009, she received first, second and third prizes from Artists Embassy International and an International Publication Award from *Atlanta Review*. Recipient of the 2007 Creekwalker Poetry Prize, she has had poems published in *Best New Poets 2008* (selected by Mark Strand), *Nimrod*, *Crab Orchard Review*, *Portland Review* and other journals and anthologies. Currently teaching at Virginia Commonwealth University in Qatar, she has lived and worked in Tibet, Macau and Thailand.

CPSIA information can be obtained at www.ICGtesting.com
Printed in the USA
LVOW110952081211

258051LV00006B/1/P